The Secret of Manpravah

Dr. Sukumar Munje

BlueRose
Publishers
New Delhi • London

First Published in January 2022

ISBN: 978-93-5472-733-7

BLUEROSE PUBLISHERS
www.bluerosepublishers.com
info@bluerosepublishers.com
+91 8882 898 898

Cover Design:
Aveek

Typographic Design:
Jyoti

Distributed by: BlueRose, Amazon, Flipkart

About Author

Dr. Sukumar Munje is the founder of Manpravah clinic and Manpravah foundation. He is a renowned psychologist and internationally certified clinical Hypnotherapist and mindfulness coach in India.

Idea of this book came up after the demand of his patients to be around him. Patients even after recovery take his appointment just to be with him. This book is all about connecting to yourself. His aim is to give people the power to analyze their own problems and understand their inner self. He wants to make his patients and others independent to understand themselves with this book.

He believes that a healthy mind is the backbone of a healthy body. So, he treats his patients in a unique , mindful way. He is not only a doctor but a mentor, friend, and guide for his patients.

Message Manpravah To You From

Thank you for choosing Manpravah. This book is like a pocket therapist, who will always be with you in your palm because it's not always possible to be with a therapist. This book will help you to keep in check with your Mental health. Staying mentally fit is a necessity in this stressful life. Our team's small efforts to reach the mass people, who can't reach us.

Manpravah thank you and respect you for privatizing Mental health.

Contents

The secret of Manpravah

Connect to yourself

Why do you need this book?

Mental health

Matters

Manpravah wheel of life

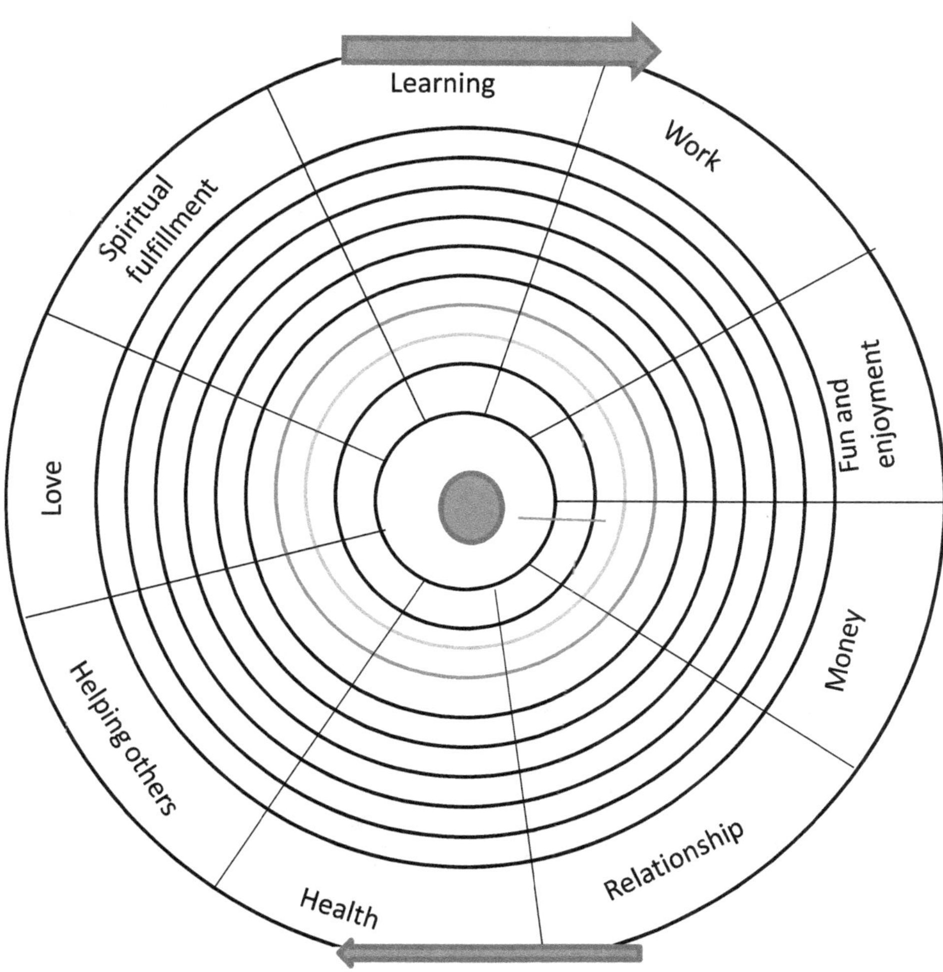

There are 10 rows in each aspect,

Inner circle shows lower satisfaction as it goes up and it shows increased satisfaction. Color each row with a different color to show how satisfied you are with each aspect of your life.

EXAMINE YOUR THOUGHT

PROBLEM	BELIEFS
Financial disaster	I am not worthy of having money.
No friends	Nobody loves me
Problems with work	I am not good enough.
Always pleasing others,	I never get my way.

Building new thoughts

I don't want to be fat.	I am lender
I don't want to be broke.	I am prosperous.
I don't want to be old.	I am eternally young.
I don't want to live here.	I now move to other places.
I don't want to have a relationship.	I have a wonderful new relationship.
I don't want to be stuck in this job.	I enjoy my work.
I don't want to have this Hair/nose / body.	I love my hair/ nose/body.
I don't want to be lonely	I am filled with love and affection.
I don't want to be unhappy.	I am joyous, happy and free.
I don't want to be sick.	I am totally healthy.

Hello Good Morning

Did you sleep well?

____

What is today's breakfast?

____

____

____

Today's Task

____

____

____

____

How are you feeling today?

____

____

____

Affirmations

____

____

____

What are you Grateful for?

____

____

____

Hello Good Morning

Did you sleep well?

____

What is today's breakfast?

____

____

____

Today's Task

____

____

____

____

How are you feeling today?

____

____

____

Affirmations

____

____

____

What are you Grateful for?

____

____

____

Hello Good Morning

Did you sleep well?

____

What is today's breakfast?

____

____

____

Today's Task

____

____

____

____

How are you feeling today?

____

____

____

Affirmations

____

____

____

What are you Grateful for?

____

____

____

Good night

You did a great job.

How are you feeling now

____

____

____

What are you grateful for?

____

____

____

How was your day?

____

____

____

Best part of the day?

____

____

____

What new thing did you learn today?

____

____

____

What one thinks you will not repeat tomorrow?

____

____

____

____

Good night
You did a great job.

How are you feeling now

____

____

____

What are you grateful for?

____

____

____

How was your day?

____

____

____

Best part of the day?

____

____

____

What new thing did you learn today?

____

____

____

What one thinks you will not repeat tomorrow?

____

____

____

____

Good night

You did a great job.

How are you feeling now

____

____

____

What are you grateful for?

____

____

____

How was your day?

____

____

____

Best part of the day?

____

____

____

What new thing did you learn today?

____

____

____

What one thinks you will not repeat tomorrow?

____

____

____

____

Hypnotherapy.

Hypnotherapy is therapeutic techniques to treat psychological disorders. In 1970 study conducted by alfred a. Barrios, this study led to acceptance of hypnosis as an extremely effective form of therapy. He found that hypnotherapy had a massive 93% success rate after only 6 sessions compared to only a 72% success rate with behavioral therapy (after 22 sessions on average), and only 38% success rate with psychotherapy (after an average of 600 sessions).

Myths and facts about Hypnotherapy.

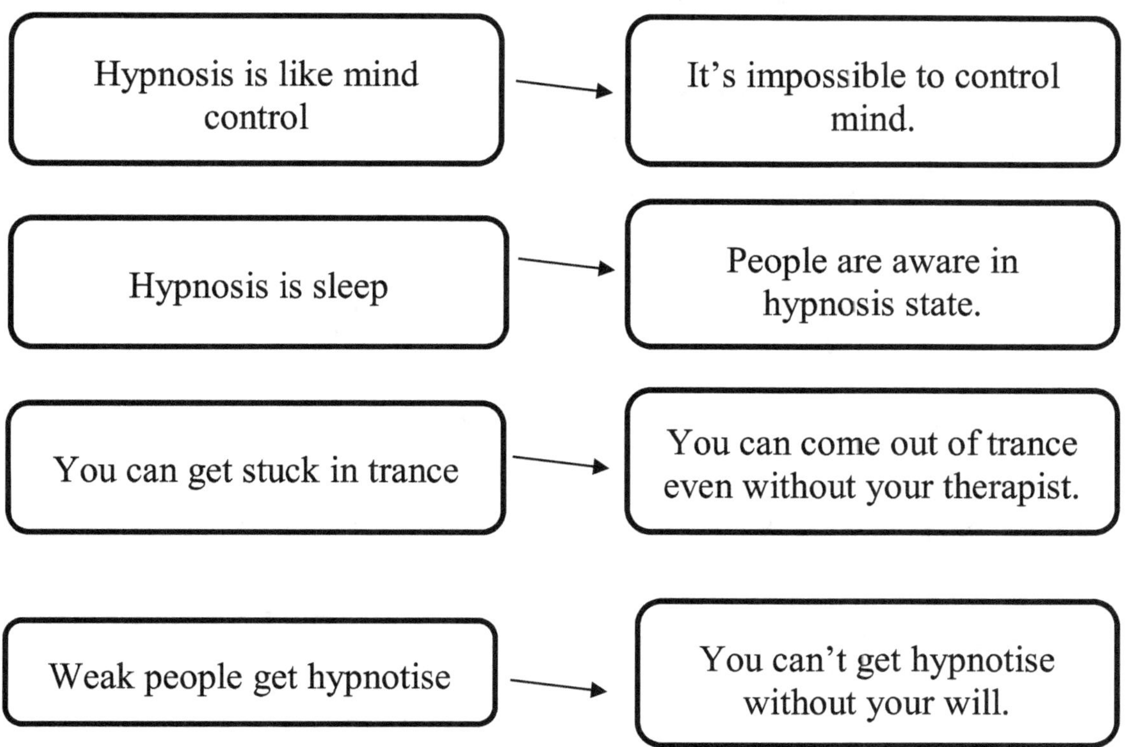

Disorders which can be treated with hypnotherapy.

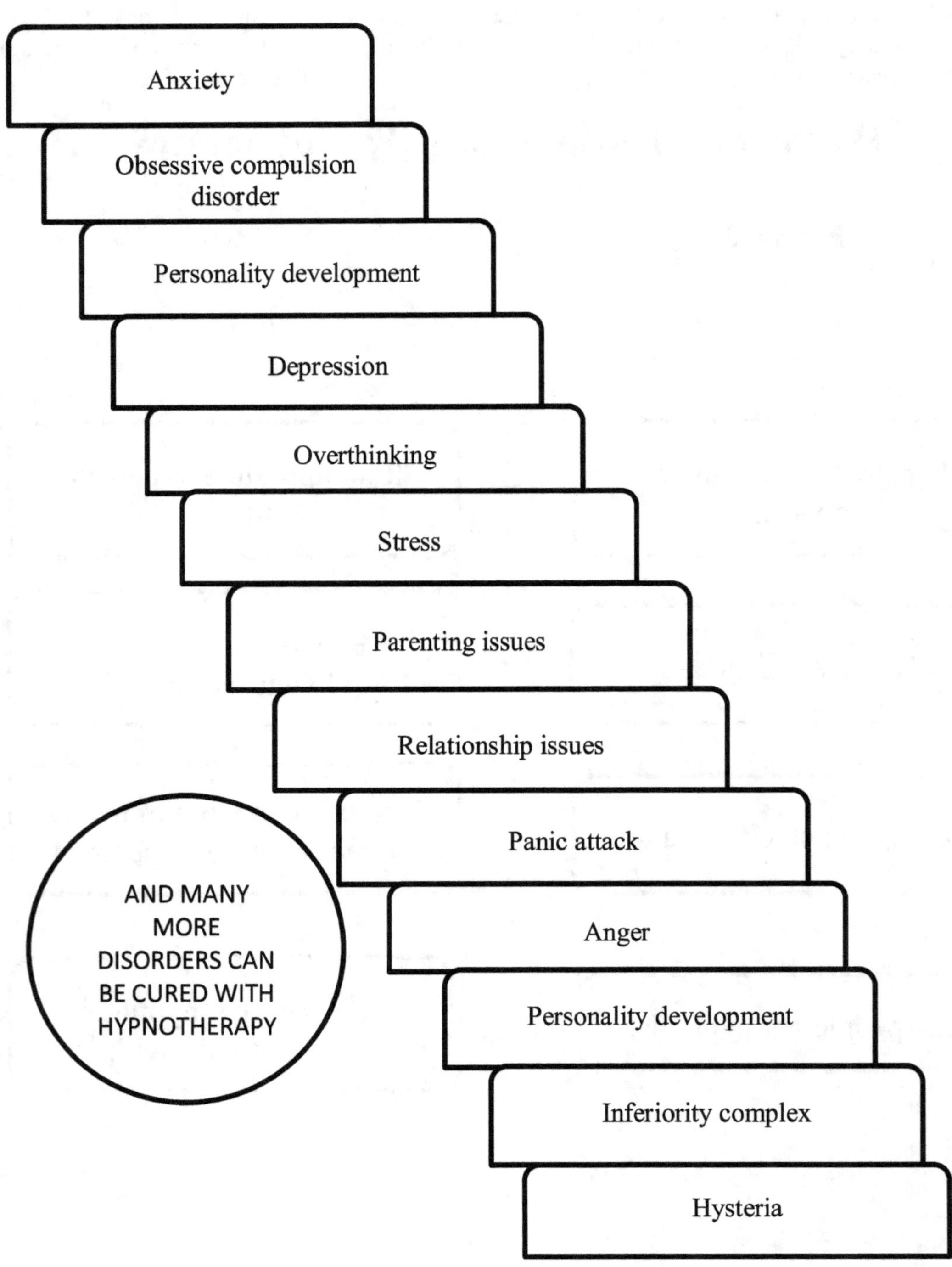

What is an Emotional Jar?

It's a magical jar to know about your emotions in depth. Write down what makes you feel down and what boosts up your good mood.

There are various things or events which trigger or boost your moods. It's important to be aware of them to enjoy or to avoid certain experiences in life.

My Emotional Jar

How do you know you need help?

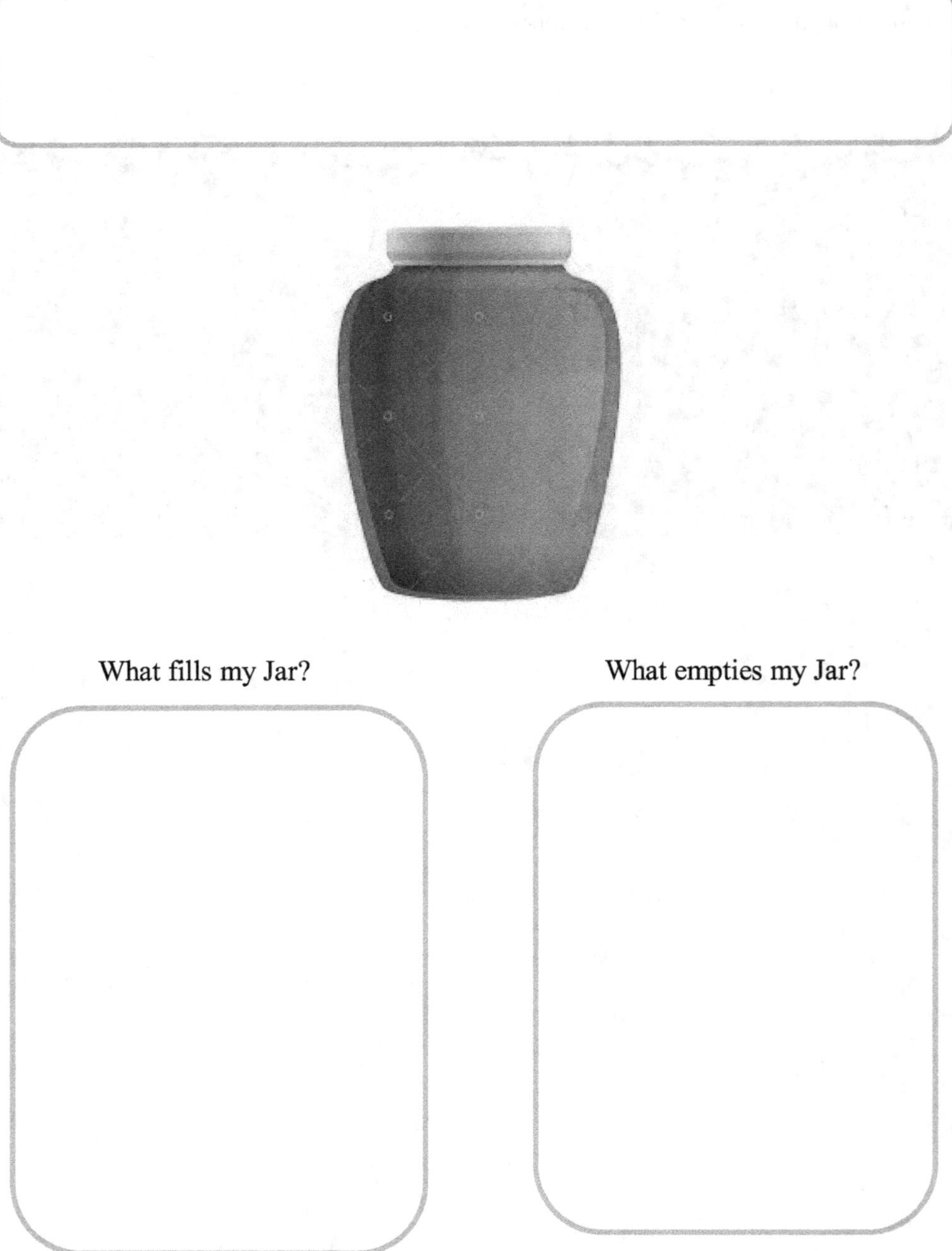

What fills my Jar?

What empties my Jar?

Habit Tracker

Why use a habit tracker?

It helps you to build new habits. It helps you to be more mindful and keep you on track. It will build consistency in you. Write one good habit which will help you to improve your lifestyle or which will make you feel good.

Name of the habit for 100 days - ___________________

Put a tick mark inside the circle after completing your task.

100 DAYS OF ....

100 DAYS OF ....

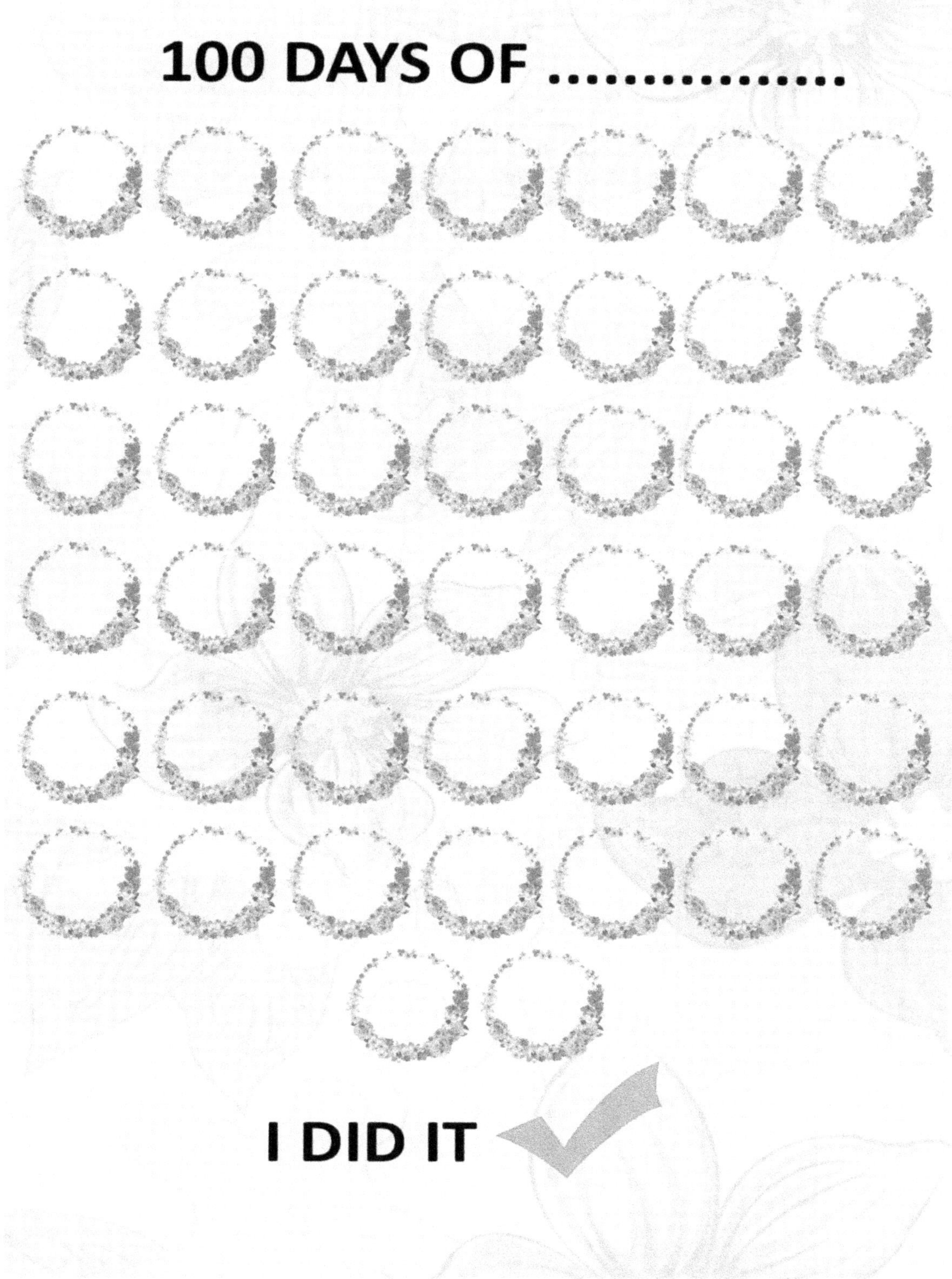

I DID IT

Meditation Time

Meditation is often defined as thinking continuously about one object of thought. We often get stuck on this definition, however, and lose the real purpose of meditation. Meditation must reveal the true nature of that object upon which we are meditating. Such revelation comes not as a thought, but as a feeling. Therefore, meditation is a process in which we shift from thinking to feeling. It is a journey from the complexity of mind to the simplicity of heart. It is for this reason that most methods of meditation involve the heart.

Color below the tree leaves after completing meditation.

Meditation Tracker

My emotions room

Write down what you feel inside that door.

Here and now

Don't dwell in the past, it has already happened, don't think about the future. It is yet to happen. To be peaceful, be in the present movement. Most of our overthinking, anxiety, stress and depression occurs because we think about the past or future. Be in the present to achieve peace.

Past	Present	Past
Anger	Calm	Anxiety
Regret	Relax	Stress
Guilt	Happy	Overthinking
Why me?	Present	Pressure
Depression	Love	What if?
Worry	Inner peace	Panic

Past   Future

MINDFULNESS ACTIVITY

Mindfulness is a superpower. It teaches you to be in the present and aware of the surroundings, being aware of what we are doing. It helps you to reduce stress, increase concentration, and enhance performance.

Activities to Perform – mindfully walking, circular walking, concentration on breathing, do every work mindfully with full attention, notice each move while working, body scan, mindful eating, body scan etc.

Mindfulness Activities

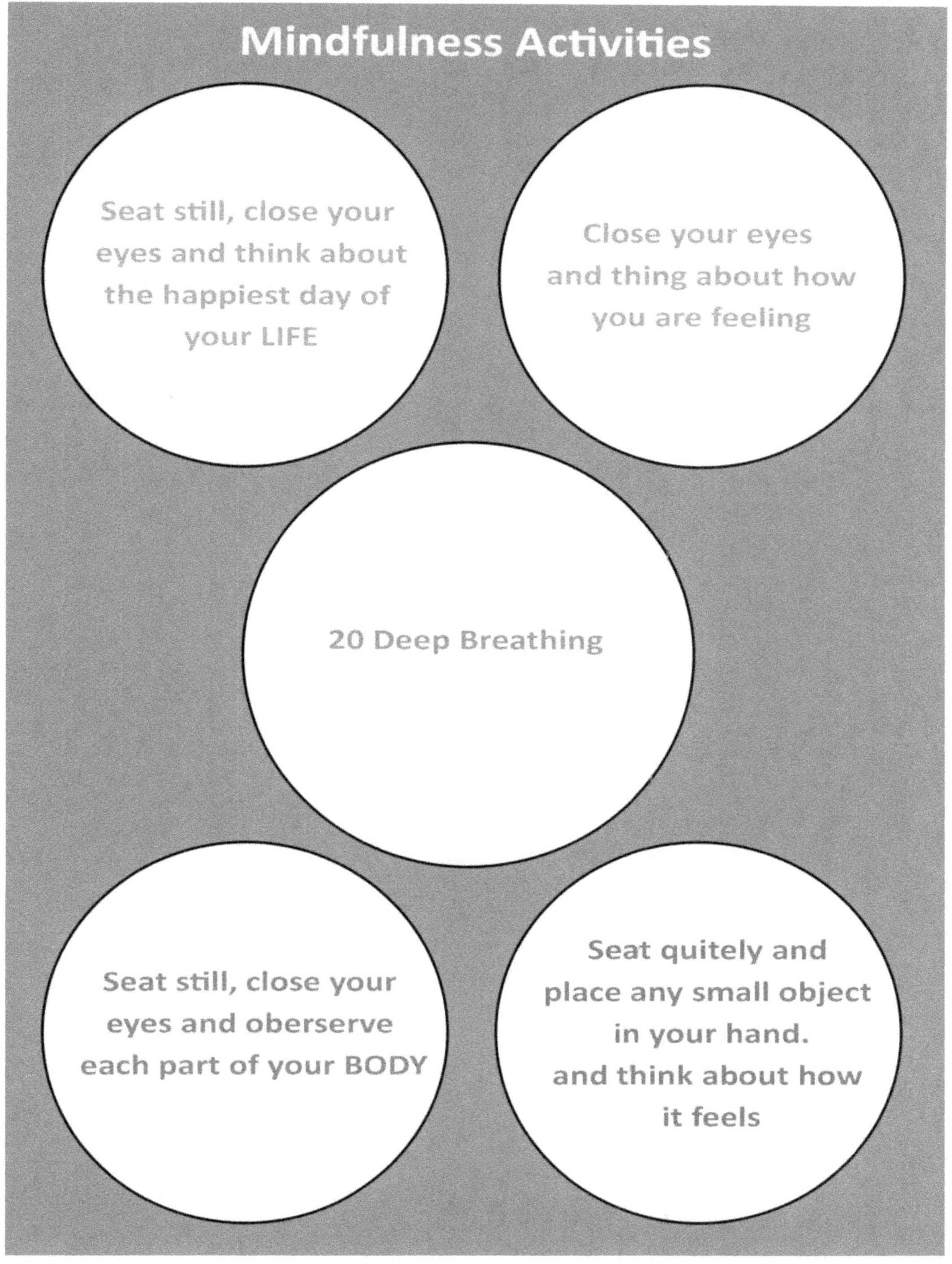

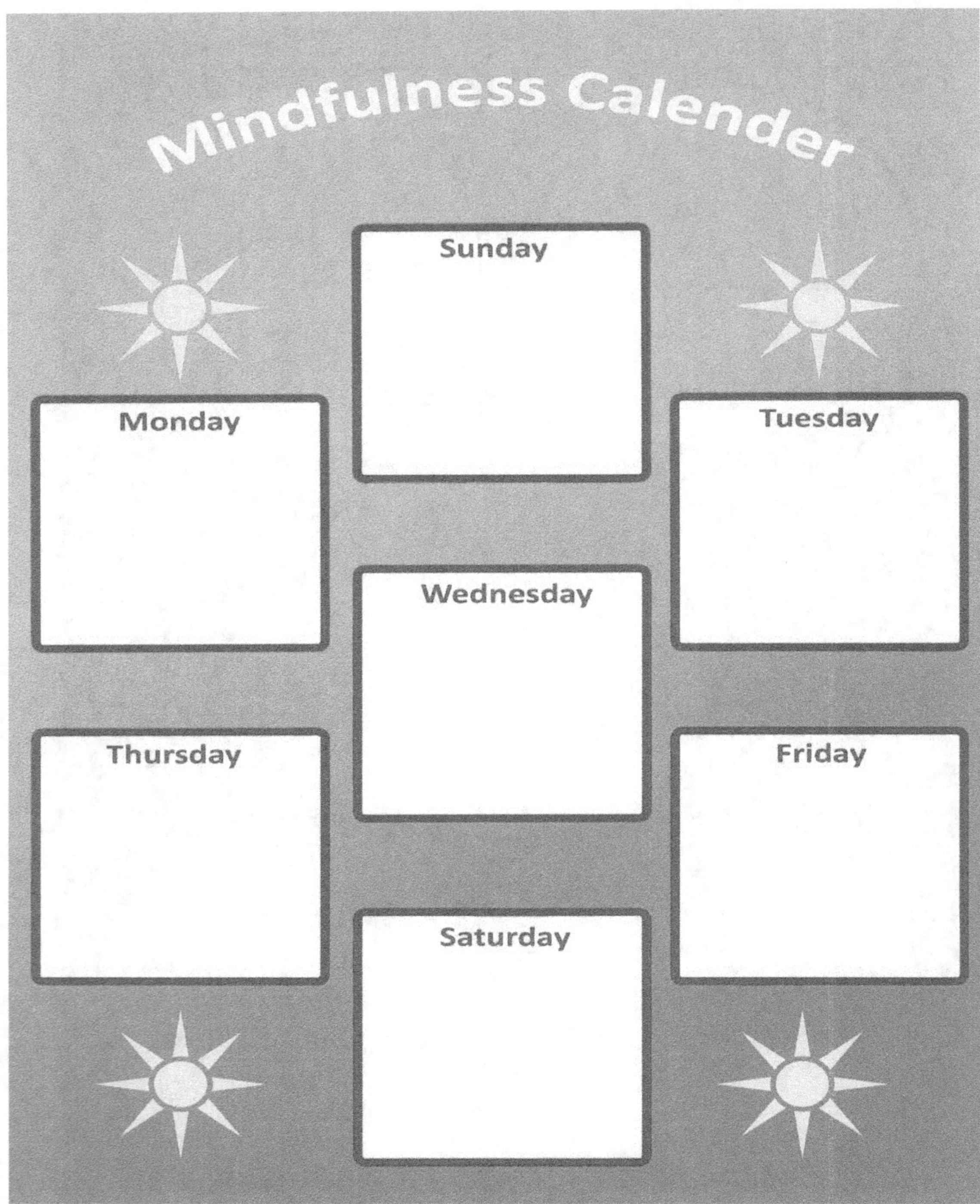

Mindfulness Calender
Sunday
Monday
Tuesday
Wednesday
Thursday
Friday
Saturday

How to eat breakfast mindfully

Mindfulness behavior is increasing awareness of present movement. Mindful eating means focusing on eating rather than multitasking. Mindful eating can improve the digestive system. It can help you to improve food habits. It teaches your brain to be in the present. Start with small tasks to be in the present movement and aware until it becomes your habit.

Baby steps to eat mindfully

- Keep all your attention on food only.
- Don't eat your food when you're stressed.
- Appreciate your food.
- Be mindful about taste, smell, texture and flavors.
- Chew thoroughly.
- Stop eating when you're full.

Rain

A Mindful tool for dealing with emotions

The situation you want to address: ___________________________

R

Recognize the emotions: ___________________________

A

Accept the emotion: ___________________________

I

Investigate it:

Your Physical sensation: ___________________________

You're Experience: ___________________________

Your thoughts: ___________________________

N

Non – identification:

____

____

____

MINDFUL LISTENING

OWL ears are very sharp. Be like an owl and listen to the voice around you.

Write down the voice you hear around you.

POSITIVE SELF TALK

Self-talk is of two types positive and negative. Negative self-talk can be very distressing and can lead to overthinking. Positive self-talk helps to improve self-esteem, confidence, reduce anxiety, depression, it helps to regulate feelings, thoughts. What you talk about with yourself gets settled in your subconscious mind.

Be gentle and kind to yourself. Write down good and positive self-talk inside the below cloud.

You can talk positive

Instruction – write down negative thoughts inside the left box and reframe it into positive ones in the right box.

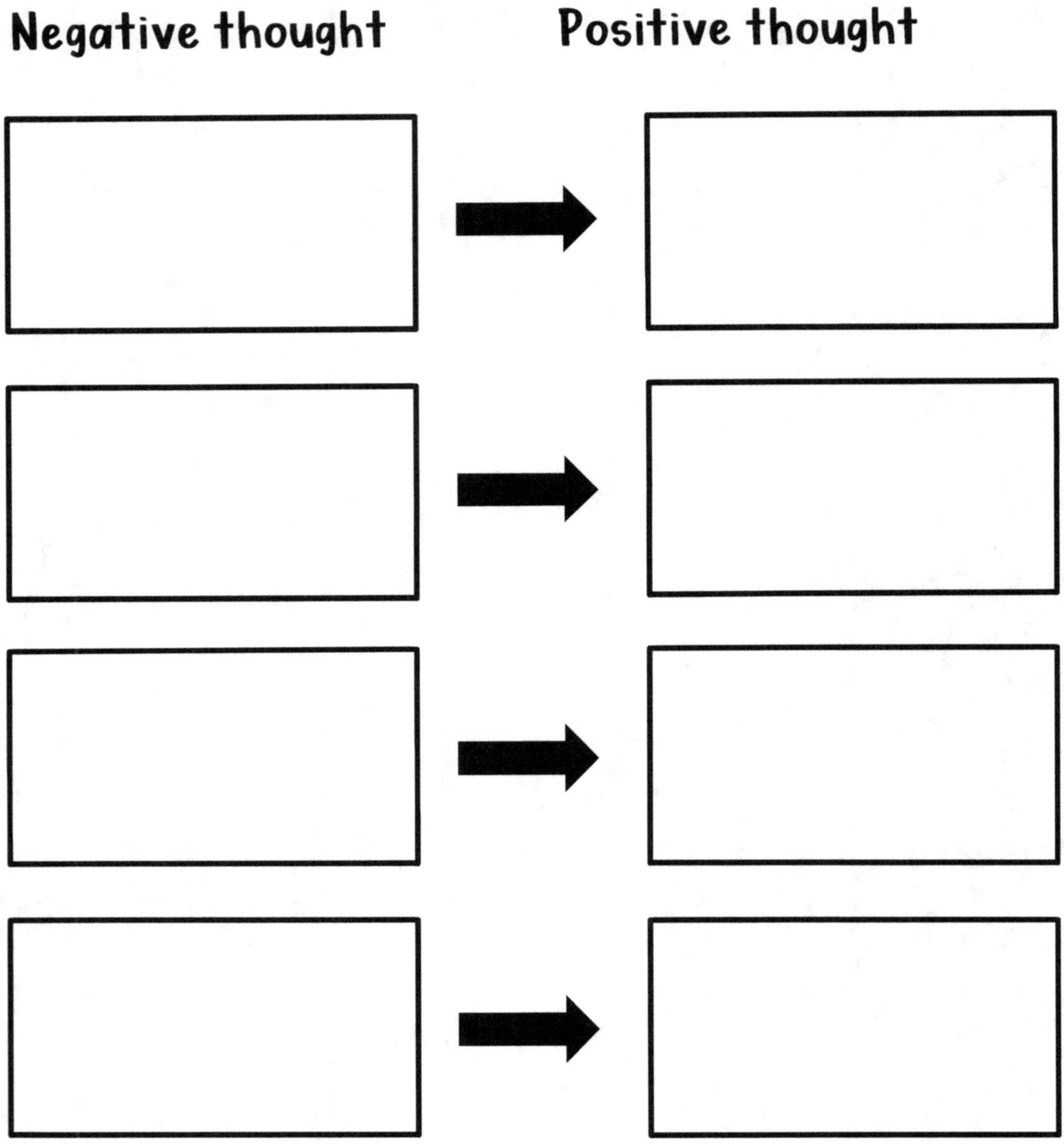

You can talk positive

Instruction – write down negative thoughts inside the left box and reframe it into positive ones in the right box.

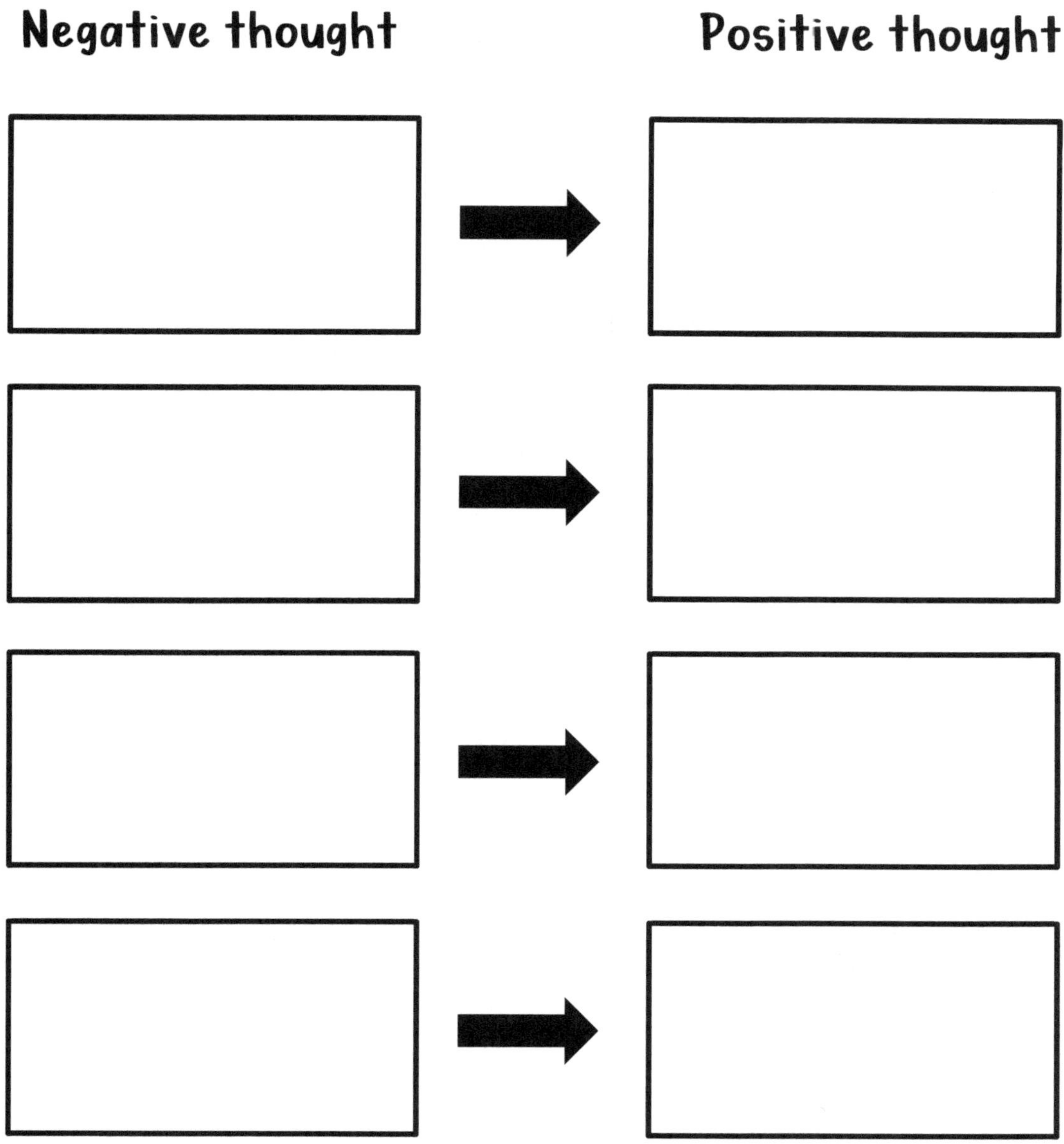

Love yourself

What do you love about yourself?

What are you proud of yourself?

What is your strength?

What is your weakness?

Stress Management

BINGO

Exercise	Breathing Exercise	Following Hobbies	Journal	Reading
Walking	Reading	Dancing	Drink less caffeine	Meditation
Progressive Relaxation	Aromatherapy	Cleaning	Positive self Talk habit	Yoga
Express Gratitude	Healthy Diet	Guided Imaginary	Mandala	Get a sunlight

Detox your thoughts

Steps to detox your thoughts

1	Time and space without technology
2	Go for a walk-in nature
3	Read good books
4	Talk with people with whom you feel good.

Today's Agenda

To do list

Priorities

Notes

TASK FOR ME TIME

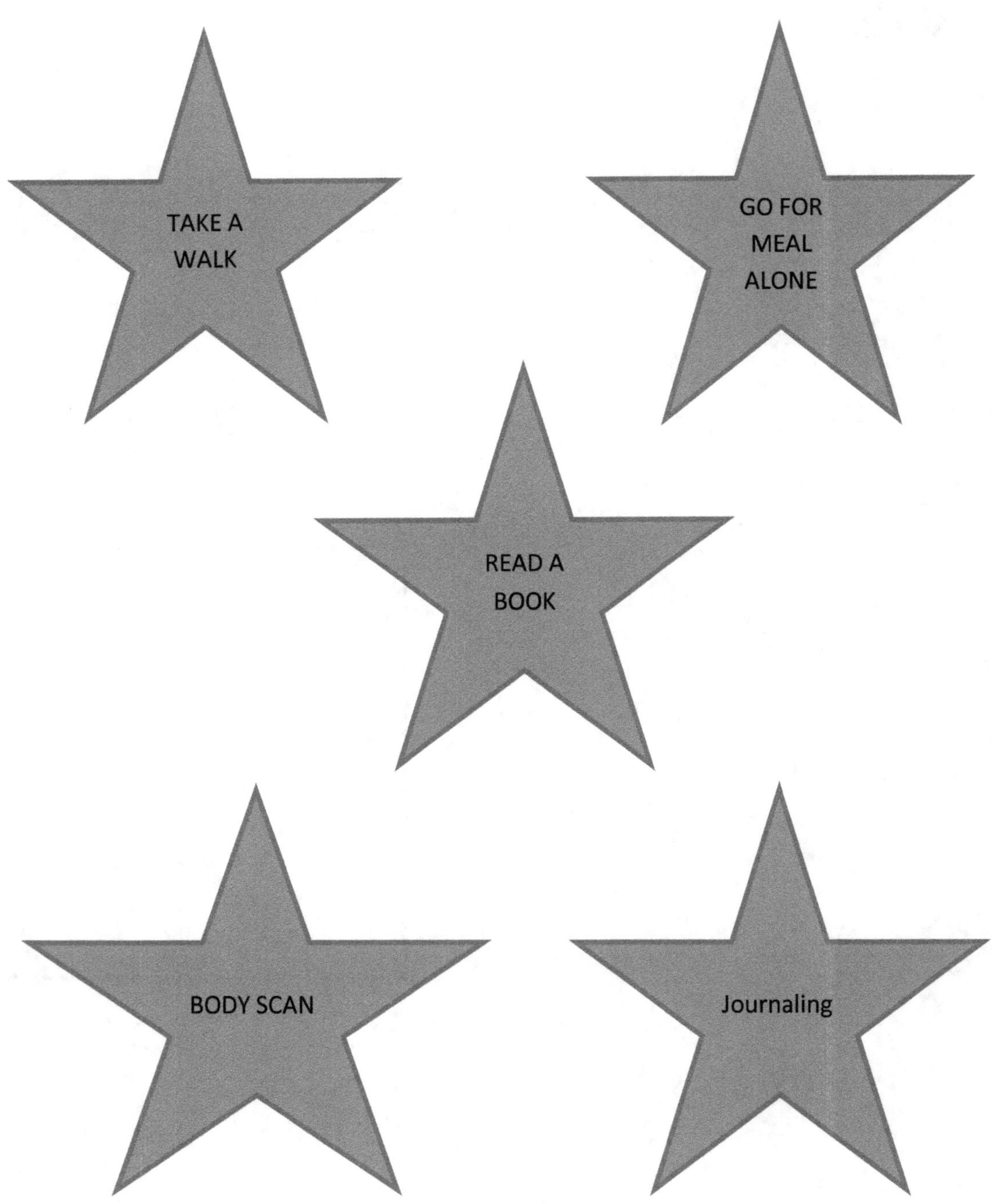

Automatic Thoughts

Trigger	Automatic thoughts	Rational thoughts
Example – I made a mistake at work.	Boss will fire me.	It's ok, it's just a small mistake. I will correct my mistakes.

GOOD NEWS

WRITE ONE GOOD NEWS DAILY.

Monday

Tuesday

Wednesday

Thursday

Friday

Saturday

Sunday

Book review

Read one book which is best for your Mental Health and write a review and what you're going to apply for your Mental Health.

Read one book which is best for your Mental Health and write a review and what you're going to apply for your Mental Health.

Write points from the book how you're going to apply in your life.

Truth about me

1)   Write down 5 good things about you?

Write down 5 good things about you?

5 What do others like about me?

2)   5 What do others dislike about me?

____

3)   Thinks I should improve
____

4)   Secret about me
____

Art Therapy

What am I proud of?   My good behavior

What am I grateful for?

LET YOUR DISTRESS OUT WITH COLOR

Connection of art therapy and reduction of stress

The main goal of art therapy is to relax. Drawing or coloring help to reduce stress and anxiety. Art therapy does not require you to be a good painter. It helps you to understand your emotions. It produces dopamine which makes you feel good.

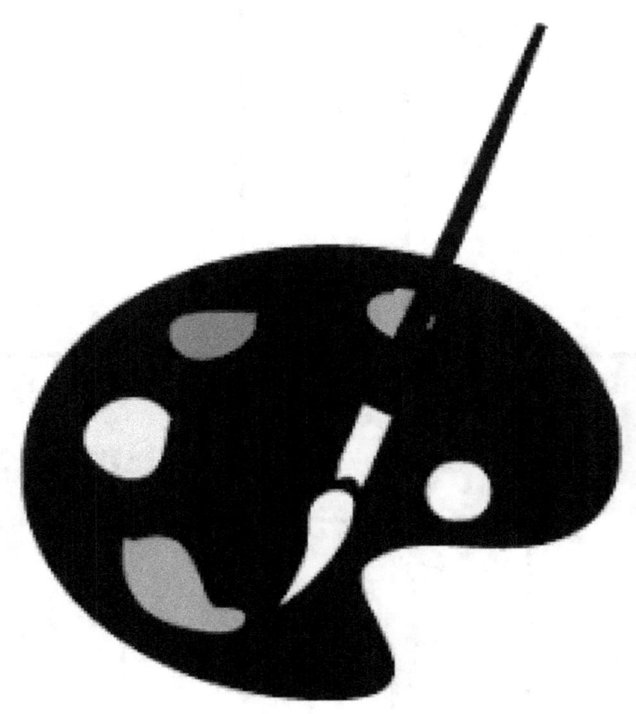

Draw the first thing that comes to your mind in the space below.

Draw Mandala and color it.

Worry worksheet

When you're worried it's easy to think about what worst will happen but in reality worries may never come true.

What is something which makes you worry?

___

What are some proving that this worry will come true?

___

What if your worry does not come true? What will happen instead?

___

What if your worry comes true? What will happen? How will you cope with it?

___

How are you feeling today?

Mood tracker

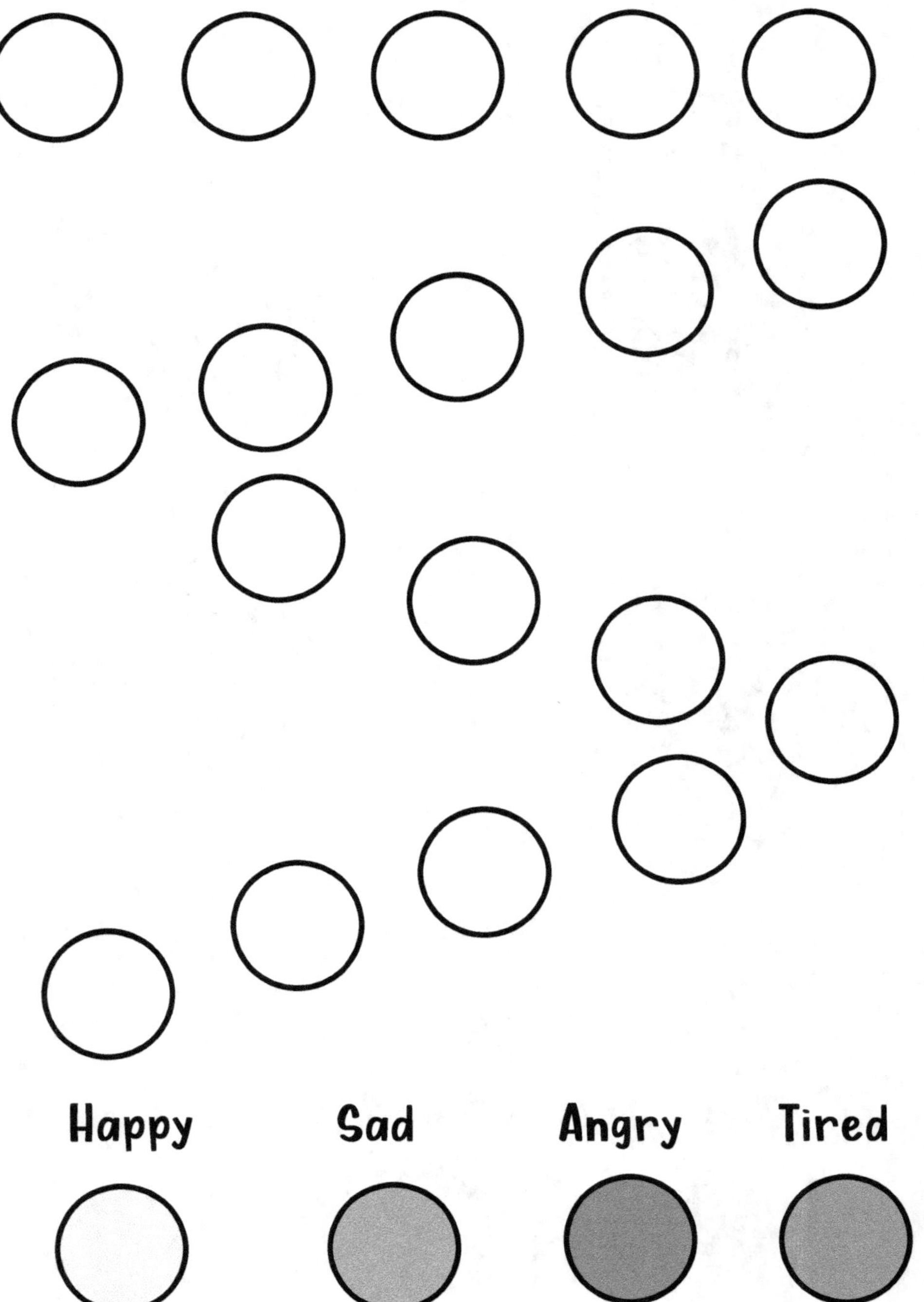

Mood analyst

Mood	Cause	Reaction

10 minutes to highlight your day

Date - ______________________________

Saw:

Heard

Tasted

Felt

Appreciated for

Worked on

Thoughts

10 minutes to highlight your day

Date - ___________________________________

Saw:

Heard

Tasted

Felt

Appreciated for

Worked on

Thoughts

10 minutes to highlight your day

Date - __________________________________

Saw:

Heard

Tasted

Felt

Appreciated for

Worked on

Thoughts

Happiness Assessment

Date - _____________________

What kind of person you are today?

____

____

____

____

____

I am happiest when?

I person that made me happy today?

3 thinks that made my mood

2 things that made me laugh

Happiness Assessment

Date - _______________________

What kind of person you are today?

____

____

____

____

____

I am happiest when?

I person that made me happy today?

3 thinks that made my mood

2 things that made me laugh

Happiness Assessment

Date - _______________________

What kind of person you are today?

____

____

____

____

____

I am happiest when?

I person that made me happy today?

3 thinks that made my mood

things that made me laugh

63

Thought cards

A new study has suggested that an average person has **6,200 thoughts per day**. Not all thoughts are important. We should learn to understand our thoughts and learn to analyze to avoid stress, anxiety and overthinking. Thought cards will help you to analyze your own thought and to check how useful or useless it is.

Thought record card

What happened?

What did you feel?

What was your thought?

What is the evidence of these thoughts?

What evidence contradicts the thought?

What's a more accurate thought?

How do you feel now?

| What happened? |
| What did I feel? |
| What was your thought? |
| What is the evidence of these thoughts? |
| What evidence contradicts the thought? |
| What's a more accurate thought? |
| How do you feel now? |

Gratitude

When we show gratitude and get back our brain releases dopamine and serotonin. ''**Thank you**'' is a small word but has a great impact on our brain and even to others. This chemical enhances our mood and makes us feel good. Expressing gratitude for good work reduces the rate of depression and stress. Gratitude is correlated with happiness. When you feel good you sleep better. Gratitude helps to strengthen relationships. Expressing gratitude can lead to more positive thoughts.

Benefits of Gratitude

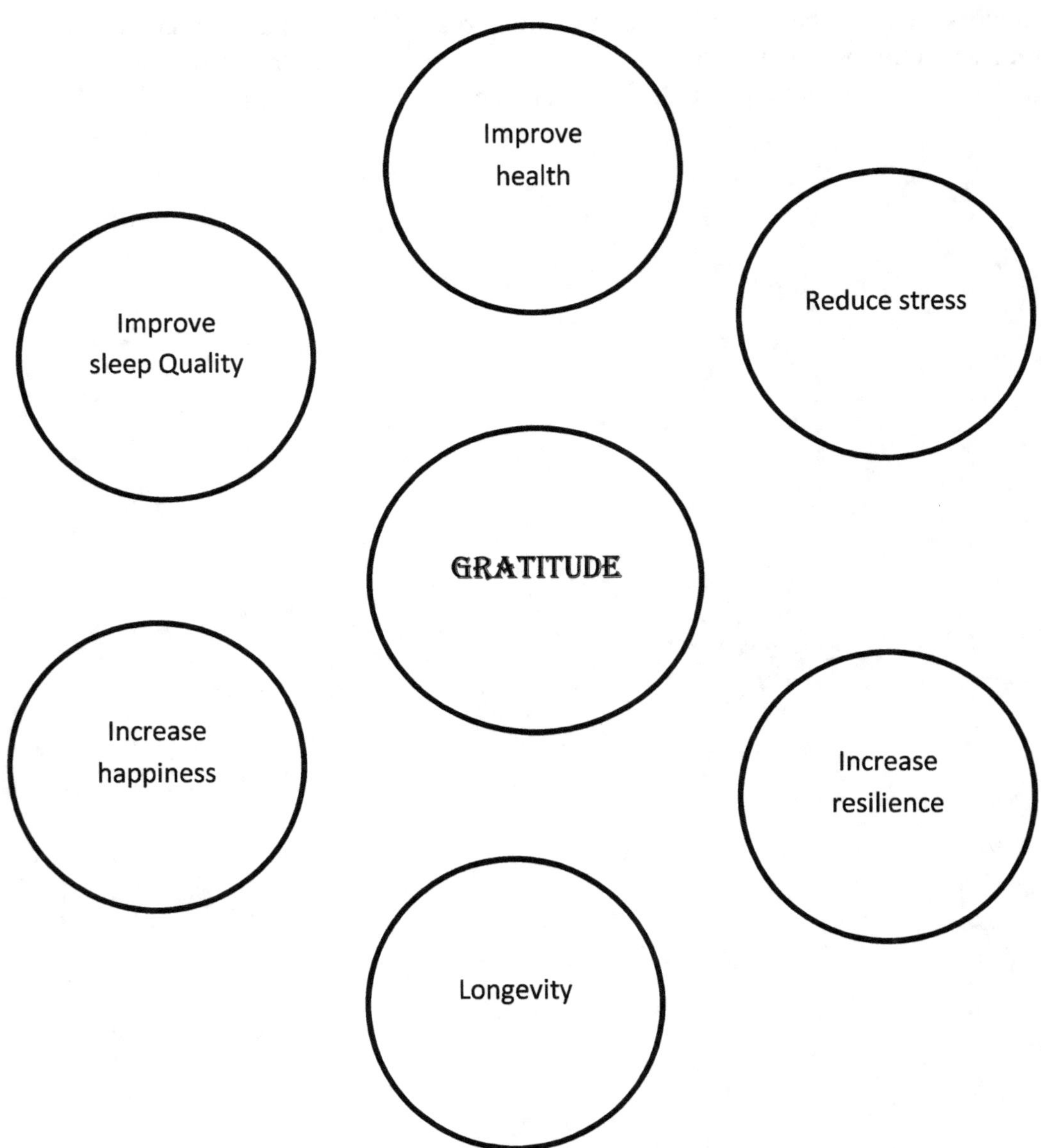

Weekly gratitude journal

Monday	
Tuesday	
Wednesday	
Thursday	
Friday	
Saturday	
Sunday	

Weekly gratitude journal

Monday	
Tuesday	
Wednesday	
Thursday	
Friday	
Saturday	
Sunday	

Reminder to yourself

Believe in yourself

Be kind to your mind

Be gentle with your emotions

It's ok to have a bad day.

Problem doesn't really define you.

Allow yourself to grow and change.

Relationship building

Relationship building is not only important with family but also outside in the society. It helps you to connect with people. Build good relationships with others and most important is to maintain the relationship. It's easy to establish a relationship but very difficult to maintain it. There are various techniques which help you to maintain relationships.

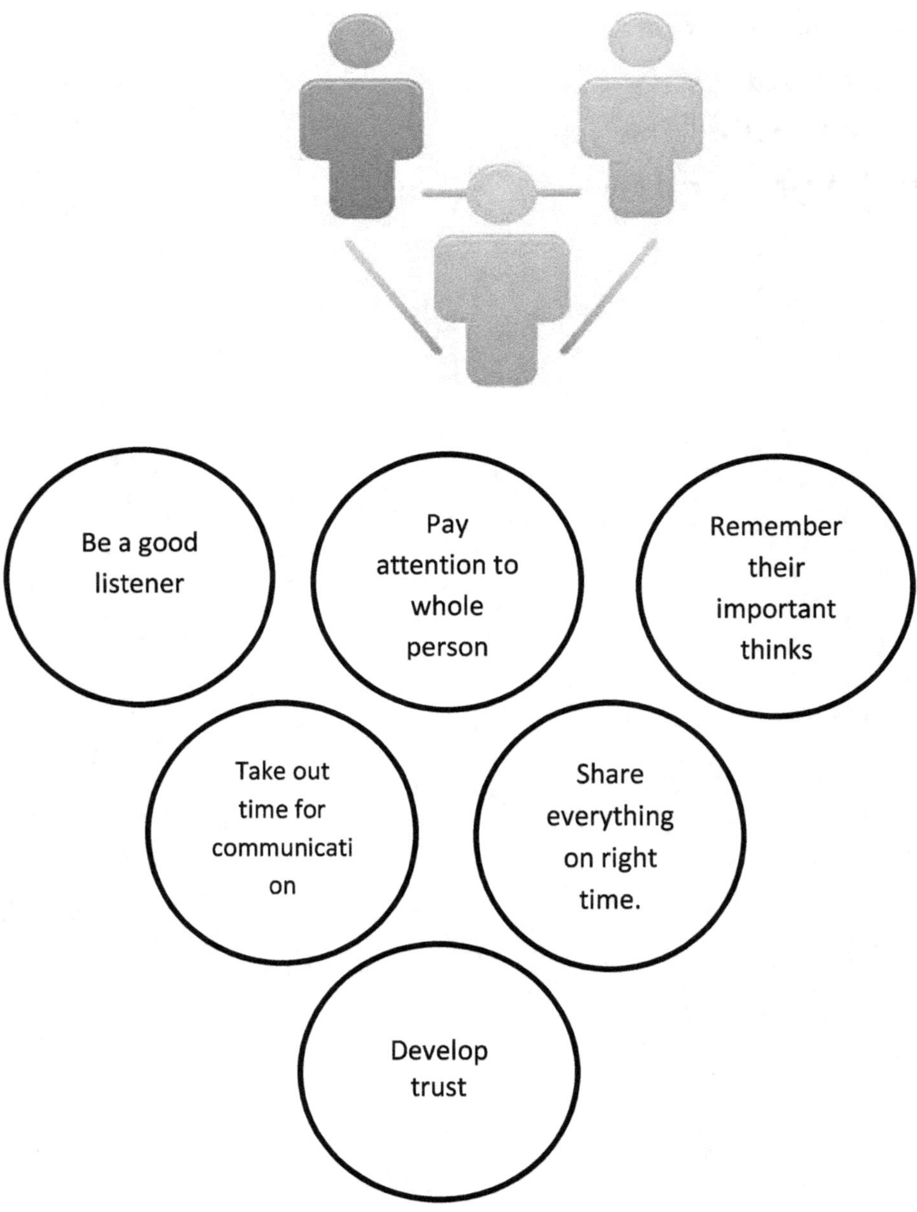

Boundaries

Boundaries are basic guidelines set by humans. It is a necessary component of human self-care.

5 types of boundaries

Emotional

Emotional boundaries are the way you protect your thoughts, wishes, feelings, perspective and ideas.

Physical

Physical boundaries are how comfortable you are with others' touch, physical needs like food, clothes, rest etc.

Mental

Mental boundary is freedom to have your own thoughts, beliefs, values and onions.

Time/ energy

Time is valuable. Setting proper time for priorities work and avoiding over commitment.

Material

Material boundaries involve setting limits on what you will share and with whom.

Boundary settings

Clear boundaries give you space to live your best life. Set your values.

Write down your values below and set what you will allow and what you will not allow.

Values

1. ______________________

2. ______________________

3. ______________________

4. ______________________

5. ______________________

What I allow

1. _______________________________
2. _______________________________
3. _______________________________
4. _______________________________
5. _______________________________

What you don't allow

1. _______________________________
2. _______________________________
3. _______________________________
4. _______________________________
5. _______________________________

What I allow but don't like.

1. _______________________________
2. _______________________________
3. _______________________________
4. _______________________________
5. _______________________________

Daily self-care

To do list

Physical needs

Affirmations

Emotional needs

Quotes

My feelings today

Water intake -

Daily self-care

To do list

Physical needs

Affirmations

Emotional needs

Quotes

My feelings today

Water intake -

Daily self-care

To do list

Affirmations

Quotes

Physical needs

Emotional needs

My feelings today

Water intake –

Manifestation

Manifestation is bringing real things in your life through conscious thoughts. It's a way to teach yourself how your thinking patterns work. It is more than thinking positive. The main and important step is gratitude. Show and express gratitude for things which you already have. When working on it you need to believe in the procedure. Our life is determined by our thoughts. Do not worry if you have negative thoughts, we all have it. We have the power to change our thoughts.

Steps for manifestation

Step one
Show gratitude for what you already have
Step two
Clarity – be clear about what you want.
Step three
Visualize – visualize what you what
Step four
Feel it – feel it while visualizing
Step five
Believe – believe that you will get what you want.
Step six
Acceptance – accept your ability to manifest what u want
Step seven
Intent – have a good intention to manifest.
Step nine
Action – act and behave like you has already manifested.
Step ten
Expectation – you have to be intent in your desire without any expectation.

Manifestation journal

Write down what you want in detail and how you will feel after receiving those things. Make sure you write everything in detail.

What you want:

Describe what you want in detail

Describe in detail how you will feel after receiving it

Goal setting

My Name -

My Goal

Starting date –

Deadline –

What steps I need to take –

What obstacles can come up –

How will you deal with it?

Forgiveness

Forgiveness is an act of kindness. Bob Enright, PhD, a psychologist at the University of Wisconsin, Madison, who pioneered the study of forgiveness three decades ago. True forgiveness goes a step further, he says, offering something positive—empathy, compassion, understanding—toward the person who hurt you. Forgiving is not a sign of weakness. Forgiveness helps you to reduce interpersonal stress. There are various benefits of forgiving like less depression, anxiety, stress, worry, improved immune system and mental health.

Forgiveness worksheet

How do you define forgiveness?

What are the pros and cons of declining to forgive the person who wronged you?

Pros	Cons

You have decided to forgive that person, so write down how things might be different if you decided to do so? write in detail

Forgiveness worksheet

How do you define forgiveness?

What are the pros and cons of declining to forgive the person who wronged you?

Pros	Cons

You have decided to forgive that person, so write down how things might be different if you decided to do so? write in detail

Anger Cycle

THOUGHT

They insulted
me

BEHAVIOUR

Urge to hit

shout

ANGER

FEELING

Anger

Frustration

BODY

Increase heart
rate, tension.

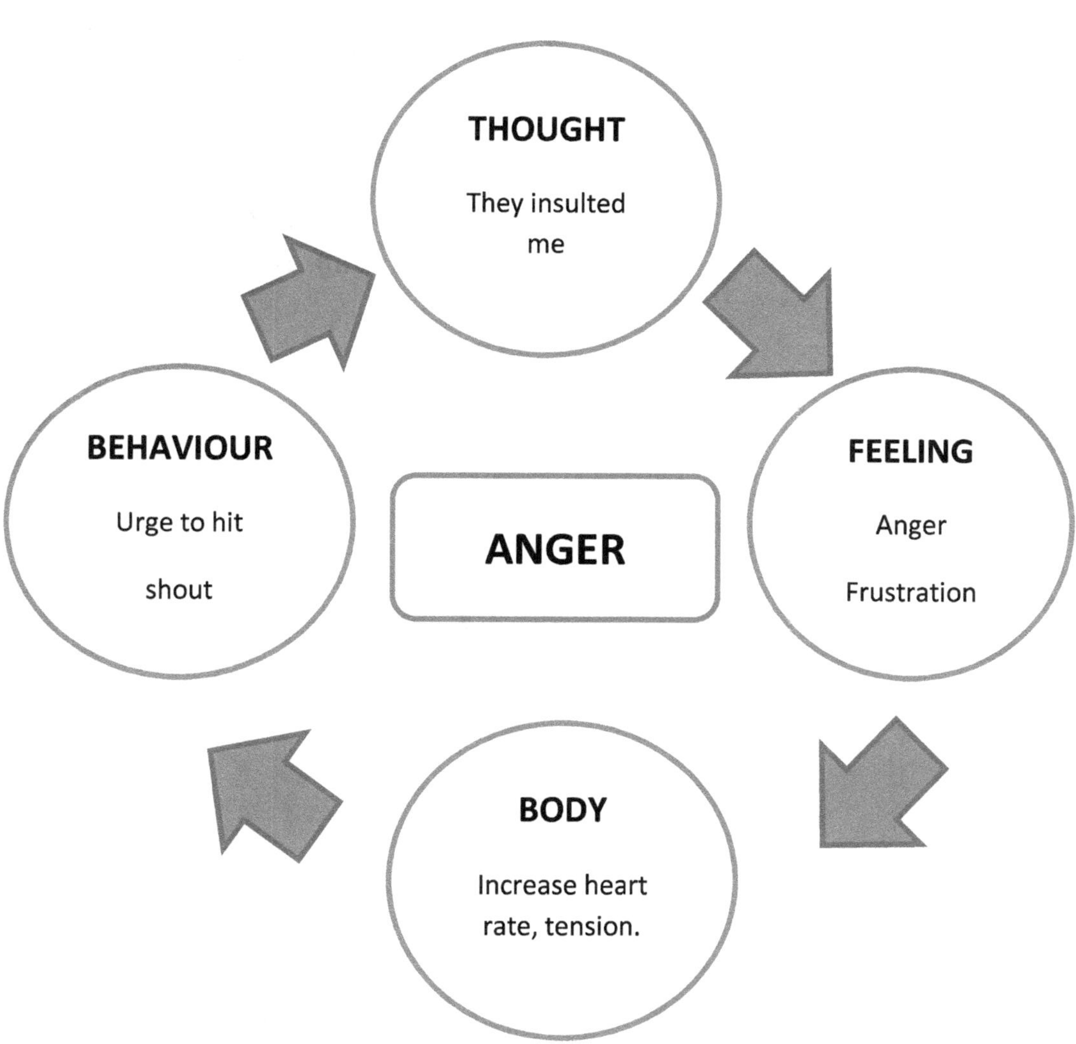

Do and don't for Anger

Do express your feeling	Don't blame others.
Recognize early sign	Don't ignore your feelings
Take time out for 10 minutes	Don't just leave; let them know you need a break.
Apply alternative to express your feelings	Don't use physical or abusive ways to express anger

Anger Map

What things do you say when you're angry?

How do you behave when you are angry?

What happens to your body when you're angry?

Other way to express your anger

What could your anger help you to achieve?

Wisdom

I trust my wisdom.
I trust your wisdom.
I respect myself.
I respect you.
I believe in myself.
I believe in yourself.
I forgive myself.
I forgive you.
I thank myself.
I thank you.
I love myself.

Positive Affirmations

I am doing my best.

I am enough

I choose to be happy and love myself today.

I am worthy

Today is going to be the best day.

I am free of worry and regrets.

I believe in myself.

I will be kind to myself and others.

I am grateful for all that I have.

I love myself.

I will be kind to my emotions.

My thoughts are filled with positivity.

I am getting better every day.

I am confident.

I am perfect just the way I am.

I accept myself.

I deserve to be happy.

I am proud of myself.

Today I am a leader.

I deserve to be loved.

Today I will overcome my fear.

Every day is a fresh start.

I can get through anything.

I feel healthy and strong today.

Prosperity affirmations

Money comes to me easily and effectively.
successful.

Wealth flows in my life.
money.

I make money every day.
wallet.

My action creates constant prosperity.
with ease.

I am a magnet to attract money.

I am confident and

I have good faith in

I have a healthy

I earn a lot of money

I respect money.

Health affirmations

 I am worthy of good health.
about my health.

I focus on positive progress.
healthy.

My body grows stronger every day.

I nourish my body with healthy choices.
strong   I deserve to feel great.
mind feels calm and relax.

I am so grateful for my body.
day.

I love to be active.
healing.

I make good decisions

My body is fit and

My focus is on positivity.

My immune system is
                                My

I feel better and better each

My body is capable of

Body scan

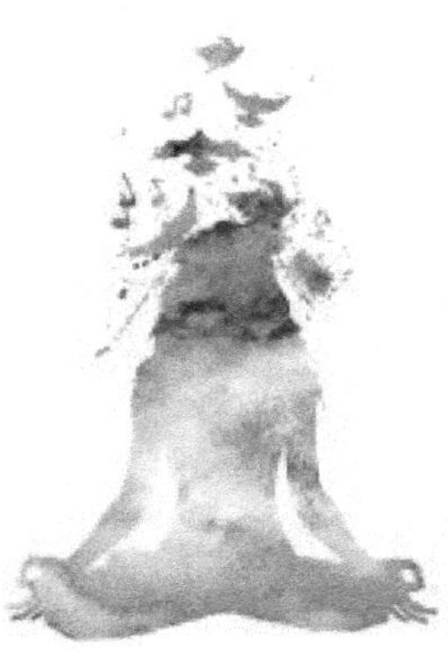

What is a body scan?

Body scan is a kind of mindful meditation to tune with your body. Focus on each part of the body and just observe it without any labelling or judging it. It helps to reduce stress, anxiety, chronic pain, insomnia and many more benefits.

Body scan Meditation steps

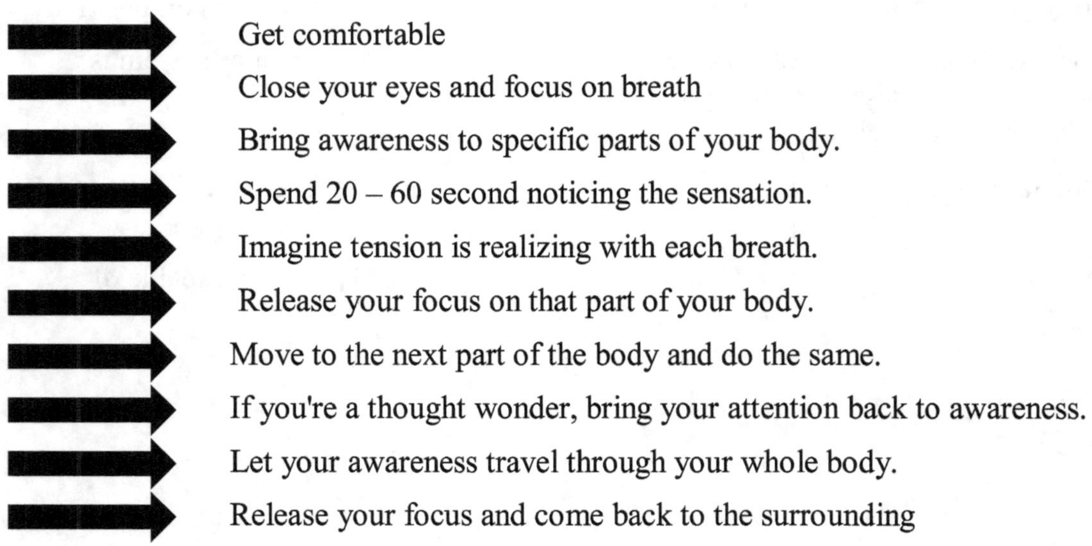

Get comfortable

Close your eyes and focus on breath

Bring awareness to specific parts of your body.

Spend 20 – 60 second noticing the sensation.

Imagine tension is realizing with each breath.

Release your focus on that part of your body.

Move to the next part of the body and do the same.

If you're a thought wonder, bring your attention back to awareness.

Let your awareness travel through your whole body.

Release your focus and come back to the surrounding

Coping skills

Coping skills is a way which you choose to deal with your stress, anxiety and other emotions. There are two types of coping skills, one is healthy and another one is unhealthy. It's good to use healthy ways for good mental health.

Healthy coping skill

1. Taking time for yourself
2. Playing sport or game
3. Positive self-talk.
4. Listening to music
5. Drawing or Painting
6. Reading a good book
7. Sharing your feelings
8. Meditation
9. Yoga
10. Exercising
11. Going for walk
12. Resolving the problem
13. Body scan meditation
14. Being in nature

Unhealthy coping skills

1. Name calling
2. Insulting
3. Yelling
4. Hurting yourself
5. Hurting others
6. Reckless behavior
7. Being passive aggressive
8. Destroying property
9. Getting revenge
10. Pretending not to care
11. Oversleeping
12. Blaming others
13. Using drugs or alcohol
14. Negative social media post
15. Emotional eating
16. Hurting others
17. Threatening

Bucket list

Everyone has their wishes. Each and every wish is beautiful. Small or big don't matter. Just write down your entire list inside the box.

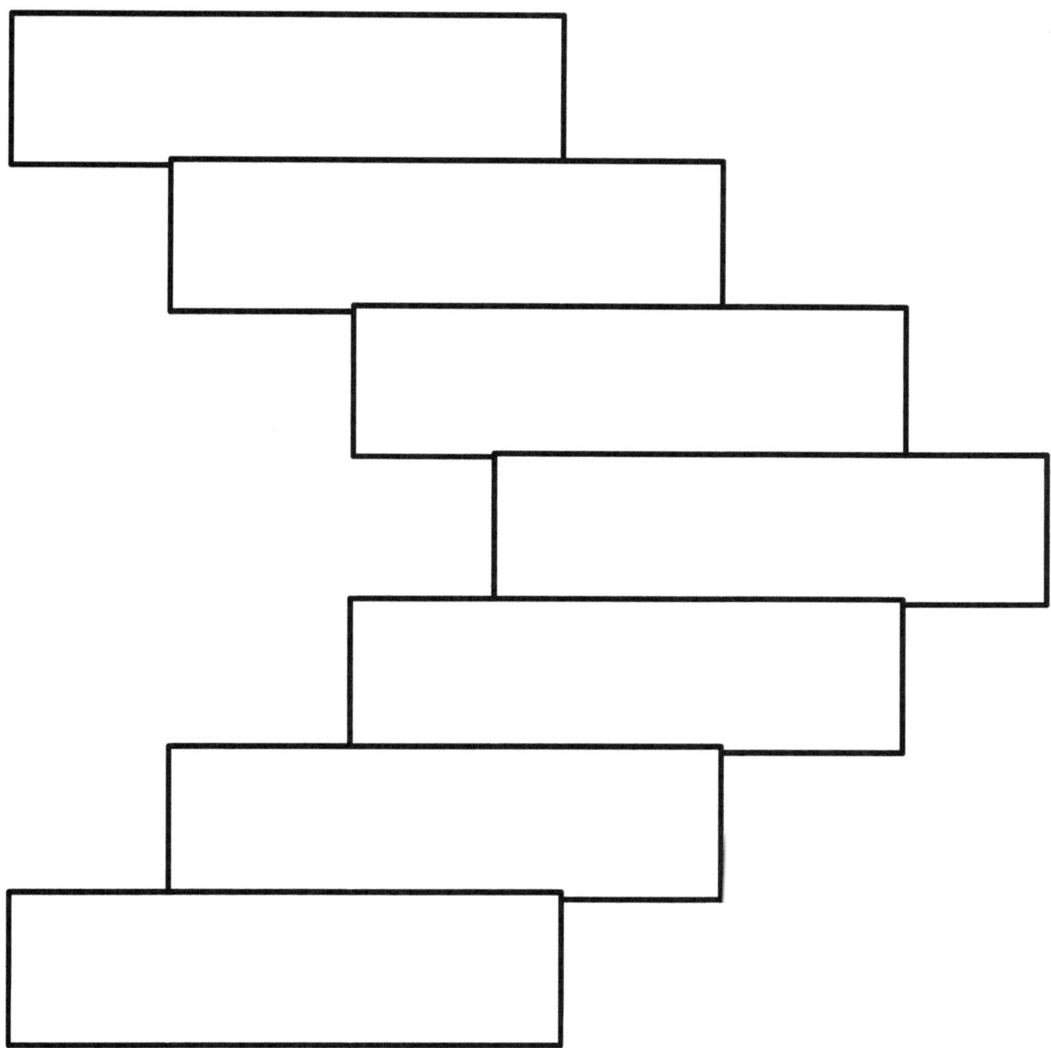

Grounding techniques

5 – 4 – 3 – 2 – 1

5 things you can see

4 things you can hear

3 things you can Feel

2 things you can smell

I thing you can taste

When you are feeling frustrated.

S   T   O   P

S   Stop

Just take a pause no matter what you're doing.

T   Take a breath

Take deep and slow breaths and come back to the present movement.

O   Observe

Just observe what is happening, for good or bad, inside or outside you.

P   Proceed

After briefly checking in with the present movement, continue whatever your work.

0.2 versions

In today's time we compare ourselves with others which lead to self-doubt, criticism etc. instead of looking into others life and personality lets work on yourself. Let's be the best version of yourself. Write down what all things can make you the best version of yourself. How can you be the best?

Progressive Muscle Relaxation (PMR)

Progressive muscle relaxation is a technique to reduce stress from the body part. Stress can create body tension. PMR helps to reduce tension in muscles and make you feel more relaxed. It helps to treat chronic pain, muscle tension, and anxiety.

Take 5 deep breaths
Squeeze your foot for 5 seconds and then relax it.
Squeeze your legs for 5 seconds and then relax it.
Squeeze your Stomach for 5 seconds and then relax it.
Squeeze your shoulder for 5 seconds and then relax it.
Squeeze your arms and hands for 5 seconds and then relax it.
Squeeze your whole body for 5 seconds and then relax it.
Take 3 deep breaths and relax yourself.

What Do You Do?

Write down what you should do instead!

WHAT HAPPENED? **WHAT SHOULD I DO?**

CRISIS PLAN

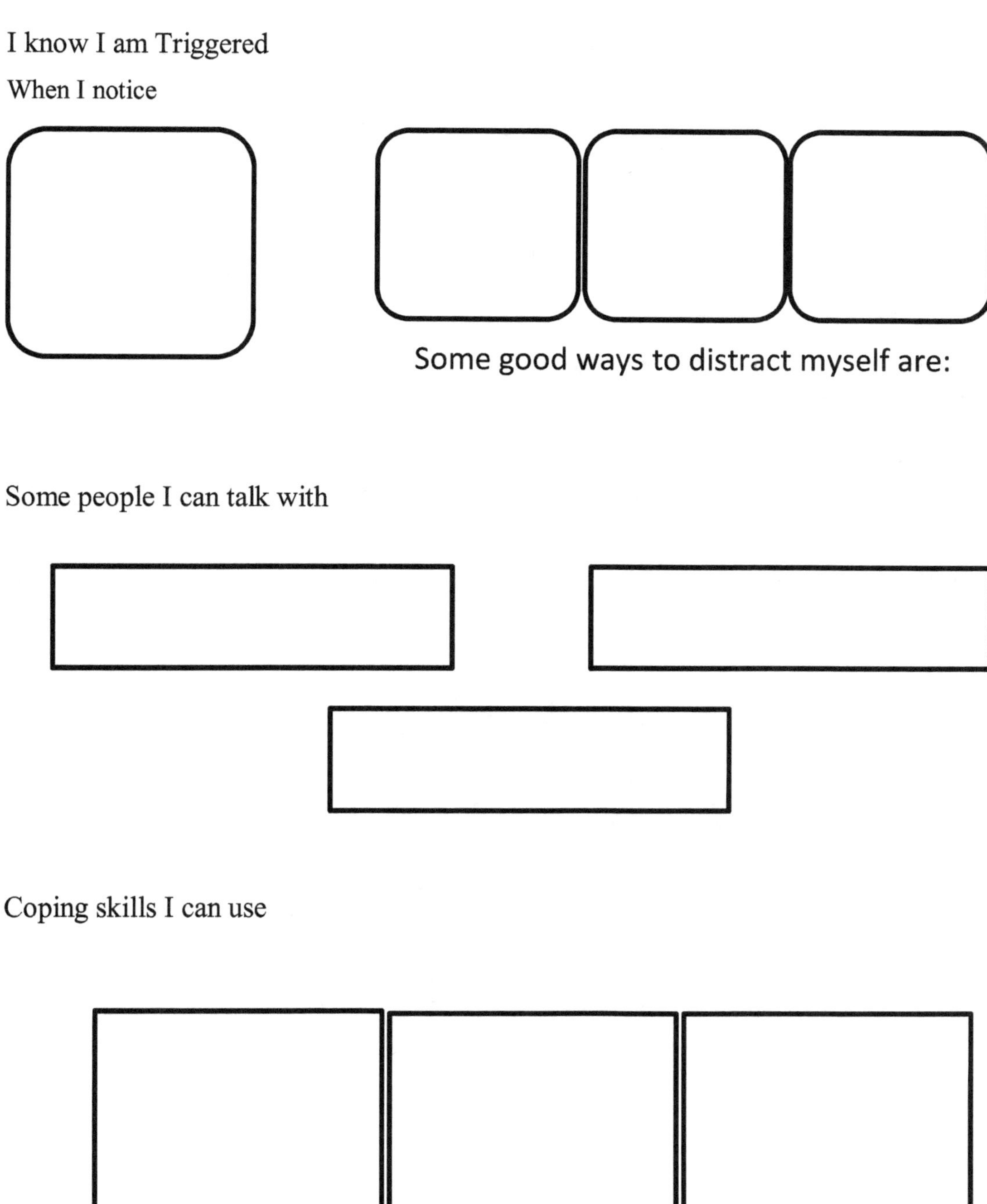

I know I am Triggered

When I notice

Some good ways to distract myself are:

Some people I can talk with

Coping skills I can use

Broken but beautiful – Japanese philosophy

It's okay to be imperfect.

Japanese philosophy says that broken things can be beautiful too. The kintsugi technique is an extension of the Japanese philosophy of wabi-sabi, which sees beauty in the incomplete and value in simplicity. Kintsugi is the art of repairing broken pots with gold or silver. Instead of hiding scars, embrace the scars.

No one is perfect, accept the imperfection and live a simple and happy life. It's important to go through tough times to know your potential. Kintsugi teaches us to celebrate our imperfections. Accepting our own imperfections will lead to peace of mind. Perfection will lead to stress and worry. Healing takes time but results can be beautiful too. In the process of healing, we can actually create something beautiful from it.

Healing yourself might take time but it will bring out the best in you.

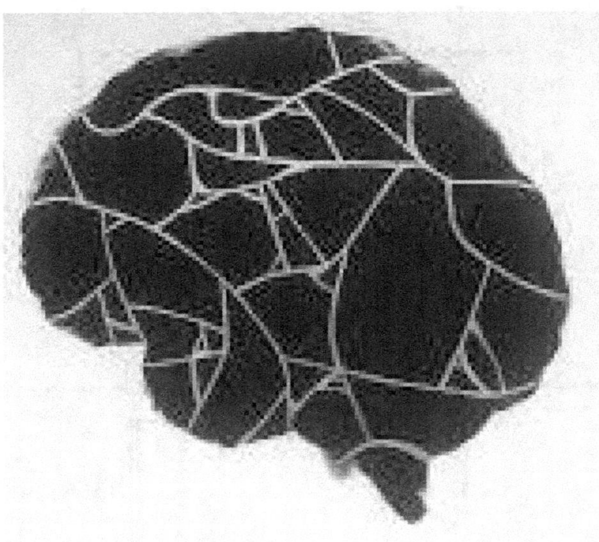

Being happy doesn't mean that everything is perfect. It means that you've decided to look beyond the imperfections. – Gerard Way

Write down inside all your flaws and accept it with grace.

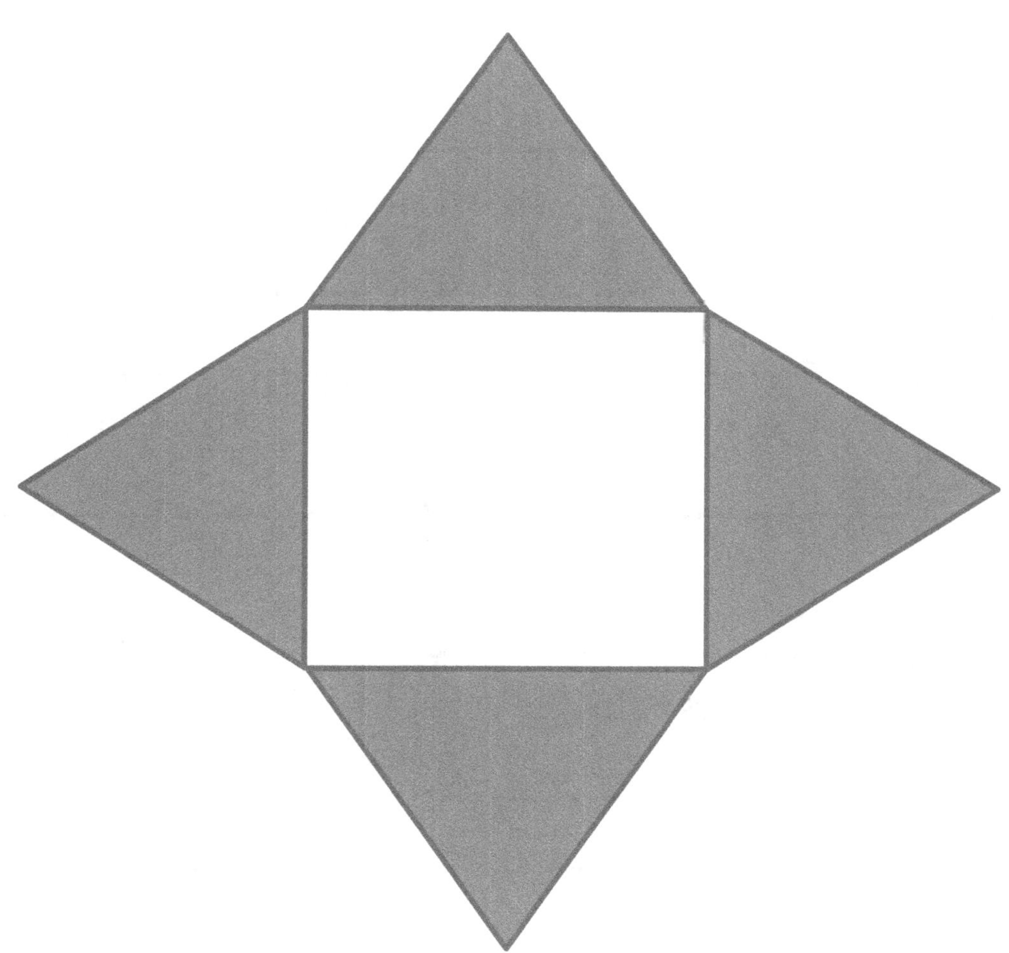

Resilience

Resilience is a process of adapting yourself to stress, trauma, threat and problem. Its mental and emotional capacity to cope in crisis situations.

Ways to build resilience

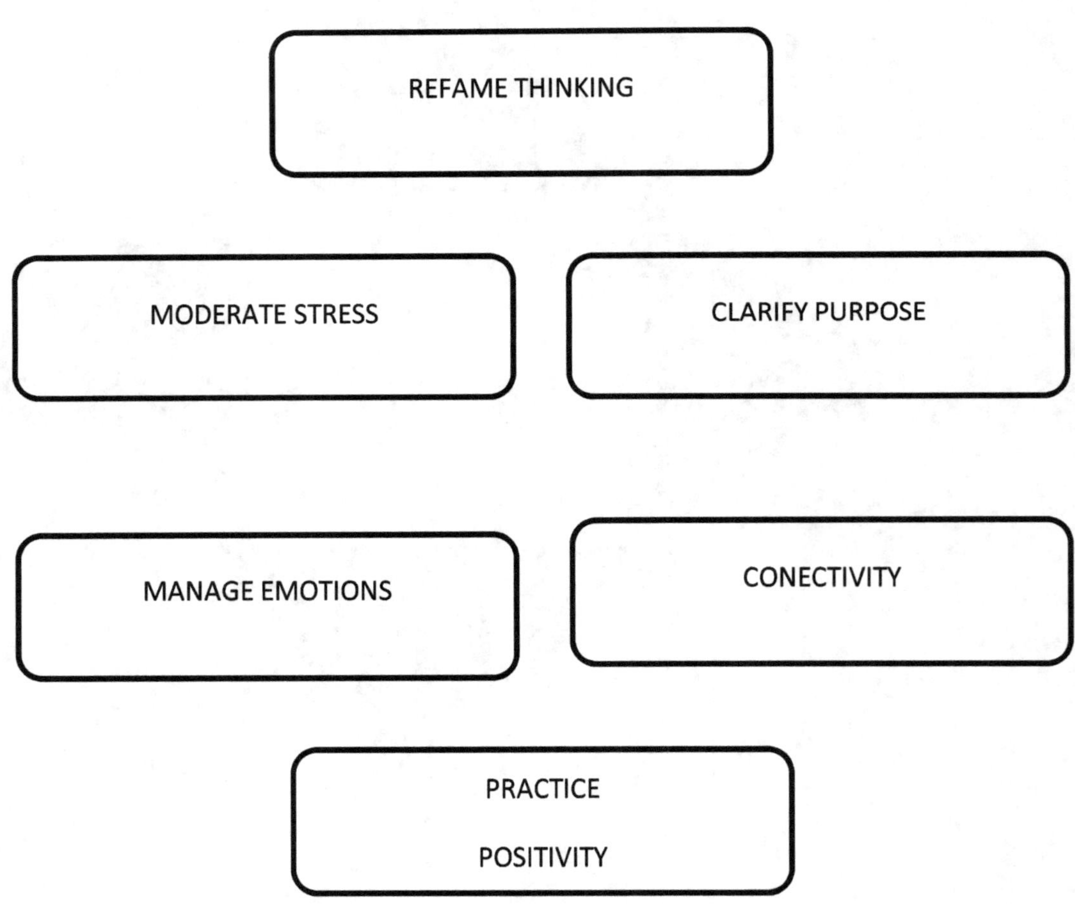

Music therapy

Music can boost up your mood. Certain music will increase happiness, motivation, can calm your mind and can even make you feel sad. Music therapy is proven therapy to deal with mental disorders.

List of music to enhance mood

- Itne shakti hame dena data.
- Ashaye song
- Zindagi pyar ka geet hai.
- I love you zindagi
- Jo jeeta yo Sikandar.
- Duniya me kitna gham hai.

Stress ratio – 1 to 10

Rate stress before music –

Rate stress after music –

Binaural beats in the alpha frequencies (8 to 13 Hz) are thought to encourage relaxation, promote positivity, and decrease anxiety.

You can listen to it for 30 minutes in the morning or at night.

Benefits of Music

Promote wellness
Express feelings
Enhance memory
Improve communication.
Manage stress.
Improve sleep
Improve mood
Lowering blood pressure.
Managing pain
Increase motivation.
Reduce muscle tension

Dr. Sukumar Munje

M.D, PhD (Hon.) In Psychology & Clinical Hypnotherapy

- [Adv Hypno, NLP] / C.C.HT
- Clinical Hypnotherapist and Psychology Counsellor
- Honoured by Health Excellence Award of Government of India for year 2020.
- Indira Gandhi Gold Medal Winner.
- Dr. APJ Abdul Kalam Excellence Award.
- India's 5000 Best MSME Award 2017 Member of Global Economic Progress and Research Association

Manpravah is one of the best Hypno-clinics in India. We offer various drug-less treatments of psychological diseases. We specialize in providing alternative therapy for depression, anxiety, stress, OCD, and even psychosis. We are known to be one of the best clinics for depression treatment by our patients.

For more details visits – www.manpravah.com

www.ingramcontent.com/pod-product-compliance
Lightning Source LLC
LaVergne TN
LVHW060559200726
843509LV00003B/159